W9-CZW-569

I WAS BORN A SLAVE

I WAS BORN A SLAVE

THE STORY OF HARRIET JACOBS

Jennifer Fleischner

with illustrations by Melanie K. Reim

The Millbrook Press
Brookfield, Connecticut

Library of Congress Cataloging-in-Publication Data

Fleischner, Jennifer.
I was born a slave : the story of Harriet Jacobs / Jennifer Fleischner ;
with illustrations by Melanie K. Reim.
p. cm.
Includes bibliographical references and index.
Summary: Traces the life of a slave who suffered mistreatment from
her master, spent years as a fugitive from slavery in North Carolina,
and was eventually released to freedom with her children.
ISBN 0-7613-0111-9 (lib. bdg.)
1. Jacobs, Harriet A. (Harriet Ann), 1813–1897—Juvenile literature.
2. Fugitive slaves—North Carolina—Edenton—Biography—Juvenile
literature. 3. Edenton (N.C.)—Biography—Juvenile literature. [1.
Jacobs, Harriet A. (Harriet Ann), 1813–1897. 2. Fugitive slaves. 3.
Afro-Americans—Biography. 4. Slavery.] I. Reim, Melanie K., ill. II.
Title.
E450.F54 1997
975.6'147—dc21   96-44350   CIP AC

Published by The Millbrook Press, Inc.
2 Old New Milford Road
Brookfield, Connecticut 06804

I WAS BORN A SLAVE

The day had been an especially exhausting one. Professor and Mrs. Botta were visiting from New York City, along with the Norwegian violinist Ole Bull. Other guests had stopped in for the day. And there were five children to look after—three girls and two boys, one of them a four-week old baby.

Harriet had been kept busy every moment—serving, scrubbing, cleaning, and tending to the children. Even now, in the evening, she was interrupted so often that she could hardly keep straight the letter she was writing.

It was a warm June night in 1857, and the ex-slave Harriet Jacobs was trying to write a letter to her dear friend, the Quaker and antislavery activist Amy Post. They had become close friends in 1849, when Harriet lived in Rochester and worked with her brother, John S. Jacobs, in his Anti-Slavery Office and Reading Room. With her brother frequently away on antislavery lecture tours, Harriet had stayed for nine months at the home of Isaac and Amy Post.

Now, at the age of forty-four, Harriet was the live-in housekeeper and nurse for the writer Nathaniel Parker Willis, and his second wife, Cornelia Grinnell Willis. The family lived in a house called Idlewild in Cornwall, New York. Harriet was fond of Mrs. Willis, and she loved the Willis children, but she missed her brother and her own two children, Joseph and Louisa, whom she could not keep with her.

Harriet shifted stiffly in her chair. Her legs were aching, as usual. Mosquitoes buzzed mercilessly around her head in the circle of lamplight that lit the dark. She could hear the children playing in a nearby room, and the merry chatter of the adults a little farther off.

Sighing, she began to read over what she'd already written.

June 21

My Dear Friend,
A heart full of thanks for your kind and welcome—letter which would have been answered immediately—but for want of time to think a moment. I would dearly love to talk with you as it would be more satisfactory—but as I cannot I

will try to explain myself on paper as well as I can—

I have My dear friend—Striven faithfully to give a true and just account of my own life in Slavery—God knows I have tried to do it in a Christian spirit—there are somethings that I might have made plainer I know—Woman can whisper—her cruel wrongs into the ear of a very dear friend—much easier than she can record them for the world to read—I have left nothing out but what I thought—the world might believe that a Slave Woman was too willing to pour out—that she might gain their sympathies. I ask nothing—I have placed myself before you to be judged as a woman whether I deserve your pity or contempt—

At this point, the letter broke off. This was when the baby, little Baily Willis, had begun crying and Harriet had gone to see what was the matter. He had only wet himself and needed changing. But then he needed to be rocked and sung to before he would fall asleep. Praying that he wouldn't wake up, Harriet had hurried back to her room.

Picking up her pen, she continued her letter:

I have another object in view—it is to come to you just as I am a poor Slave Mother—not to tell you

what I have heard but what I have seen—and
what I have suffered—and if there is any
sympathy to give—let it be given to the
thousands—of Slave Mothers that are still in
bondage—suffering far more than I have—let it
plead for their helpless Children that they may
enjoy the same liberties that my Children now
enjoy—. . . .

Harriet paused to blink away the tears that were gathering in her eyes. Then, laying down her pen, she pulled open the bottom drawer of the desk at which she was writing. Inside lay a handwritten manuscript, tied with a blue ribbon. She lifted it with two hands, and held it up to the light.

Here it was—the story of her life—written by herself, just as she had lived it. Everything she felt she could say about her life as a slave girl in North Carolina and her escape was in that manuscript. She knew that many Northerners would not believe her story. But they had no idea what slavery was really like—nobody could who had not been a slave. No doubt, they would decide that her account of how she hid for seven years in her grandmother's house before running North was a crazy woman's fantasy. But it was all true—every single word.

A creaking floorboard just outside the door gave warning, and Harriet quickly slipped the manuscript back into its hiding place. No one in the Willis household knew that Harriet was writing a book about her life. She believed that Mr. Willis would not approve of such a thing. For four years Harriet had written secretly at night, after her long workdays were done.

Harriet held her breath, listening for another step or a knock, but none came. Still, she was surprised to find herself breathing heavily and trembling all over. What was the matter with her? She lifted her pen, trying to steady her hand. This was exactly how she felt when, hiding in the crawl space above her grandmother's kitchen, she would hear the heavy footfall of her master, Dr. Norcom, in the room below. "Have you heard from Harriet?" he would demand to know. "You tell her she'd better come home, or else I'll send her children to the plantation, and she knows what will happen to them there."

The memory of her master's voice crushed out all other thoughts. How he still had the power to hurt her!

But as she had done many times before, Harriet Jacobs fought off thoughts of her master. She turned her mind to the projects at hand. She finished her letter and sealed it into an envelope. Then she reopened her private drawer, took out her precious manuscript, and set to work.

Edenton sits at the head of a bay leading out to Albemarle Sound, in the northeastern corner of North

Carolina. In the early nineteenth century, the town was a grid of streets, with roads stretching out to the surrounding plantations and farms.

About 1813, a little girl was born in Edenton to two slaves, Delilah and Elijah. (Until recently, Elijah's name was thought to be Daniel.) Delilah was the slave of an Edenton innkeeper and his wife, named John Horniblow and Elizabeth Pritchard Horniblow. Elijah was owned by Dr. Andrew Knox, whose plantation stood several miles northeast of Edenton. Both Delilah and Elijah were mulattoes, people of mixed-race background. They named their daughter Harriet. Jacobs, the surname (last name) she would use, came from a poor white farmer, Henry Jacobs, a neighbor of Andrew Knox, who was probably Elijah's father.

For the first several years of her life, Harriet Jacobs lived with her parents and her younger brother, John, in a house in Edenton. Living together, they felt almost like a free family. Elijah was a highly skilled carpenter, and he arranged with his mistress that, for the price of two hundred dollars a year, he would be allowed to hire himself out at his trade. His reputation was so widespread that he was called to be head workman on jobs for buildings being constructed miles away.

Harriet and John (who was two years younger than his sister) were also raised by their maternal grandmother, Molly Horniblow. Like many slaves, Molly was the child of a white slaveholder and slave mother. Molly's father, a South Carolina planter, had died during the Revolutionary War, leaving Molly's mother and three children free. But on their journey south to St. Augustine, Florida, where they had relatives, the mother and children were recaptured as slaves and sold to different buyers. That was how Molly came to Edenton, as she was bought by John Horniblow, the Edenton innkeeper.

Molly was a valuable slave to the Horniblows. She nursed their children as if they were her own. But she could never forget that while the white children were free, hers were slaves. Longing to be able to buy freedom for her five children, Molly began a business as a baker. She would bake crackers and cakes late at night after working all day for her mistress, then sell her goods to her Edenton neighbors. With her profits, she clothed herself and her children and saved up a little money every year.

But her plans to secure freedom for her children were soon dashed. When John Horniblow died, he left a will that divided Molly's children among the Horniblow heirs. Delilah, Harriet's mother, became the property of one of the Horniblow daughters, Margaret.

As a child, Harriet was grateful to her good grandmother, whose gifts of cakes and preserves were a loving comfort and source of nourishment for her and her brother in hard times. And she loved her gentle mother and her proud father, who taught his children feelings of independence.

But when Harriet was six and John four, their mother died; and it was then, as Harriet would write, that

> *for the first time, I learned, by the talk around me, that I was a slave. My mother's mistress* [Margaret] *was the daughter of my grandmother's mistress. She was the foster sister of my mother; they were both nourished at my grandmother's breast. In fact, my mother had been weaned at three months old, that the babe of the mistress might obtain sufficient food. They played together as children; and, when they became women, my mother was a most faithful servant to her whiter foster sister. On her death-bed her mistress promised that her children should never suffer for anything; and during her lifetime she kept her word.*

For the six years following her mother's death, Harriet lived with Margaret Horniblow. She remembered these as happy years. She would sit by her mistress's side, sewing for hours at a time. If her mistress thought she looked tired, she would be sent outside to run and play. Harriet remembered gathering flowers and berries to decorate her mistress's room. Margaret Horniblow also taught Harriet to read and write, which was a rare privilege for a slave. During those years, as Harriet would recall, she

had a "heart as free from care as that of any free-born child."

But for a slave, such days were not likely to last. In 1825, Margaret Horniblow took sick. This was a frightening time for Harriet. What would become of her if her mistress died? Her father, who had remarried a free black woman and had a son, had just been ordered back to his master's plantation, miles outside of Edenton. And as a slave, her grandmother had no say in what would become of her grandchild.

Harriet loved her mistress and prayed that she would get well. But her prayers went unheeded, and her mistress died. Margaret Horniblow was buried in the church graveyard in Edenton, and Harriet spent many dejected hours weeping at her grave.

After her mistress died, Harriet was sent to live with her grandmother to await the reading of the will. From sorrow, her feelings turned to hope. She was certain that her mistress had kept her promise to her mother to free her and John. All of their relatives and neighbors were sure of it. Margaret Horniblow had so loved Delilah. She would never knowingly break her promise to her dying foster sister—to the dying slave mother.

But when the will was read, Harriet had her first bitter taste of the value of a slaveholder's word to a slave. Her mistress had given "my negro girl Harriet" to her sister's three-year-old daughter, along with "my bureau & work table & their contents." At the same time, Margaret willed John to her mother, Elizabeth Pritchard Horniblow, who was their grandmother Molly's mistress. Although Margaret Horniblow had treated the Jacobs children with kindness, she had still considered Harriet and John as *things*.

In her autobiography, Harriet Jacobs describes the following scene.

John's mistress and their father, Elijah, happened to call for John at the same time. Uncertain as to whom he should obey first, John decided to go to his mistress. His father was furious.

"You are *my* child," he told his son, "and when I call you, you should come immediately, if you have to pass through fire and water."

What could a child do—a child who was at once a son and brother, or a daughter and sister, with thoughts and feelings—and yet a child who was a slave, considered to be somebody's property, an object without feelings and thoughts at all? And how would a father or mother feel who had no say at all in their child's fate?

To be treated as a slave saddened and angered Elijah deeply. He had been forced back to the Knox plantation, where he was prevented from practicing his craft as a carpenter and where he was no longer able to be a father to his children. These changes were hard blows to his spirit, and he grew depressed.

Meanwhile, Harriet and John worked as slaves in the Norcom household: Harriet belonged to little Mary Mathilda Norcom and John was "on loan" to her father, Dr. James Norcom, who used him as a shop-boy and physician's assistant.

The Norcoms lived on Eden Alley, the next street over from where Molly Horniblow lived. Dr. Norcom's medical office was nearby, on King Street, next to the county courthouse and jail. In addition to being a physician, Dr. Norcom was a well-to-do, slaveholding man. He owned several town lots and a few farms in the surrounding county, and at least nineteen slaves.

Dr. and Mrs. Norcom were cruel masters. They gave their slaves barely anything to eat, and the slaves had to make due with whatever scraps they could find in the kitchen. Often hungry, Harriet would stop by her grandmother's house while doing errands for her mistress in order to get enough to eat. Her grandmother would stand by the gate and hand her a bit of food quickly, so as not to risk making Harriet late.

Masters and mistresses were also expected to supply their slaves with clothes, and in this the Norcoms were as stingy as they were with food. Mrs. Norcom gave Harriet one coarse linsey-woolsey dress to wear every winter, but no new shoes.

One snowy February day, when Harriet passed by her grandmother's, her grandmother gave her a pair of new shoes to replace her worn-out ones. But when Harriet wore them into Mrs. Norcom's room, the creaking noise they made on the floor irritated Mrs. Norcom.

"What is that noise?" she asked, crossly.

"My new shoes," Harriet answered.

"Well, take them off," her mistress replied, "and if you put them on again, I'll throw them into the fire."

Harriet removed her new shoes carefully, along with her stockings. Mrs. Norcom then sent her on another long errand. Harriet's bare feet tingled as she raced through the snow.

Dr. and Mrs. Norcom were especially spiteful in their cruelty. If the Sunday dinner was not served on time, Mrs. Norcom would wait until it was all dished out, then spit in the kettles and pans that had been used for the cooking to prevent her slaves from scraping any leftover gravy or other crumbs from the pots for their meals. If Dr. Norcom didn't like the taste of a dish, he would either order the cook to be whipped or force her to eat every mouthful in front of him. Once, when a sickly pet dog, whom the slaves regarded as a nuisance, refused to eat the mush the cook had been ordered to make for him, Dr. Norcom claimed that it had not been properly prepared, and forced the cook to eat it all herself.

Harsher punishments were also commonplace. Soon after she came to the Norcom household, Harriet saw Dr. Norcom order a slave to be tied up to a ceiling beam in the work house, so that his feet would fall just short of reaching the ground. He was left there until Dr. Norcom, who was taking his tea, came to whip him. Harriet lay all night listening in horror to the poor man's cries and groans. The slaves never knew for certain why this man was punished.

About a year after she went to the Norcoms, Harriet's grandmother met her in the street one day.

"Come with me," she said, drawing the girl aside. Harriet knew right away that something was wrong. "My child," her grandmother then told her, "your father is dead."

Dead! Harriet thought. She had not even known he was sick! She felt angry and betrayed. She believed in God, and she felt that He had taken her mother, mistress, and father away from her. Her grandmother tried to comfort her with the thought that their loved ones had been spared from worse times to come. But it was cold comfort to Harriet.

She returned alone to the Norcoms' house. She thought about her father all night. When the morning came, she intended to go to her father's house. As she was about to leave, Mrs. Norcom ordered her to go fetch some flowers for an evening party she was planning. Instead of spending her day beside her father's body, Harriet was obliged to spend the day picking flowers and weaving them into festive wreaths for her hateful mistress. But on the next day, she was allowed to see her father buried in the graveyard next to her mother.

After their father's death, Harriet and John tried to cheer themselves up by imagining that someday they might be free. Harriet hoped that when they were older, they would be able to hire out their time and earn money to buy their freedom. But John declared that he would never buy his freedom; that he would take it when he could.

John's fierceness was a little frightening. But it was bold and exhilarating, and Harriet half-believed her brother was right to think this way.

According to the Norcoms' way of thinking, Harriet was a pampered slave. She still had her grandmother, brother, and other relatives, including aunts and uncles, who helped to look after her. Unlike a plantation hand, she lived in the Norcoms' house, sleeping in a room with her great-aunt Betty, and her duties often included playing with the young Norcom children. And she had never been whipped.

But Harriet's view of her situation was entirely different. She would rather have been a starving pauper than a slave. Then things got worse.

When Harriet was a teenager, Dr. Norcom began to find excuses to be alone with her. He followed her wherever she went, on her errands or when she was visiting her parents' graves. He would complain of the heat in the tea room, order his supper to be brought out on the piazza, and tell Harriet to stand by and brush away the flies while he ate. He wanted the fifteen-year-old Harriet to agree to become his lover. He was about fifty years old at the time.

One day Dr. Norcom announced that he wanted his youngest daughter, Elizabeth Hannah, who was then about four, to sleep in his room. It was considered necessary that a servant be on hand to attend to the child should she awaken. Dr. Norcom decided that Harriet would be that servant, and sleep in his room as the child's nurse.

The first night, Harriet managed to avoid going to the doctor's room. She stayed with her great aunt, whose room had become a refuge from the doctor. It seemed that the only place to which the doctor would not pursue her was her great-aunt's room. Even he respected the old woman, who had served in his family for many years. Also, as a married man and doctor, he wanted to keep up the appearance of respectability. Although it was well known throughout the town that Dr. Norcom was the father of several slaves, such things were common in the slavery South, and few people objected openly, since the master's slave children were considered to be additions to his property.

But many other people suffered privately from this practice. Harriet was tormented by Dr. Norcom's intentions. He hounded her with promises, threats, pleadings, and denunciations.

"Did I not take you into the house, and make you the companion of my own children?" he would say. "Have I ever treated you like a negro? I have never allowed you to be punished, not even to please your mistress. And this is the recompense I get, you ungrateful girl!"

But Harriet knew that Dr. Norcom had his own reasons for shielding her from punishment. She saw the jealous rage in her mistress's heart whenever Mrs. Norcom looked at her. Mrs. Norcom was the doctor's second wife and many years younger than he. She seemed powerless to control his behavior, so she took out her misery and anger on the defenseless girl.

When Mrs. Norcom discovered her husband's scheme to have Harriet sleep in his room, she flew into a fury. She then sent for Harriet to come to her room.

"Did you know you were to sleep in the doctor's room?" she asked.

"Yes, ma'am."

"Who told you?"

"My master."

"Will you answer truly all the questions I ask?"

"Yes, ma'am."

"Tell me, then, as you hope to be forgiven, are you innocent of what I have accused you?"

"I am."

Mrs. Norcom then handed Harriet a Bible, made her kiss it and lay her hand on her heart and swear to tell the truth, then asked Harriet to tell her all that had happened between the master and herself.

Harriet did as she was ordered, but she saw that instead of enlisting Mrs. Norcom's sympathy, she was infuriating her further. Mrs. Norcom wept with anger and wounded pride. Harriet would have given anything to have Mrs. Norcom's pity and compassion. But she only became a greater target for her wrath.

Afterward, Mrs. Norcom made Harriet sleep in a small room next to her own. But this gave no rest to either of them. Sometimes the mistress would creep into Harriet's room and stand over her bed, watching her. Other times, she would bend over and whisper words into the sleeping girl's ear as if she were her husband, to hear what Harriet would say. If Harriet awoke, she would glide away, and the next morning ask Harriet who it was she had been talking to in her sleep. In time, Harriet grew fearful for her life.

Dr. Norcom tried to use his wife's persecution of Harriet to his own advantage. "Poor child! Don't cry! don't cry!" he would soothe. "I will make peace for you with your mistress. Only let me arrange matters in my own way. Poor, foolish girl! You don't know what is for your own good. I would cherish you. I would make a lady of you. Now go, and think of all I have promised you."

Alone with this double torment, Harriet longed to confide in someone who might help her. She wanted to tell her grandmother all her troubles. But Dr. Norcom threatened to punish her if she dared to do this. Harriet herself felt ashamed to confess to her grandmother what was bothering her, and this also made her hang back. Her brother tried to comfort her without knowing what was wrong, for she didn't dare tell him. The cook and the other slaves knew what was happening and silently pitied Harriet. They feared being punished for even speaking of it at all.

In her agony, Harriet saw how different were the fates of the slave child and the white child:

I once saw two beautiful children playing together. One was a fair white child; the other was her slave, and also her sister. When I saw them embracing each other, and heard their joyous laughter, I turned sadly away from the lovely sight. I foresaw the inevitable blight that would fall on the little slave girl's heart. I knew how soon her laughter would be changed to sighs. . . .

Harriet did share her suffering with one other person. A number of free black families lived in Edenton. In one of them was a young man who as a child had played with Harriet and John. He now lived and worked as a carpenter in the neighborhood where Harriet lived. They often met in the street, where they would walk a little way, talking. In this way, they fell in love.

They talked frequently about marrying. But because Harriet was a slave, their marriage would not be recognized by law. They could be separated at the whim of her master, and their children would be slaves. Besides, to marry, they needed Dr. Norcom's permission, which Harriet knew they were unlikely to get. He had sometimes watched them together from his window, and had never failed to punish Harriet in some petty way out of jealousy and spite.

The young couple realized that the only way they could get married was to persuade Dr. Norcom to sell Harriet to the young man. But how were they to do that? Dr. Norcom could hardly be expected to give up Harriet to another man, especially a free black man whom Harriet loved. And though Mrs. Norcom might want to be rid of the girl, she would never do anything to promote her happiness.

Seeing her granddaughter in such despair broke Molly's heart. Molly was now a free woman, having been emancipated two years earlier by her mistress. She had managed to buy one of her own sons to make him free. She owned her own house. But Dr. Norcom would never sell Harriet to her.

It occurred to Molly that their neighbor, a woman who was a good friend of Dr. Norcom's and who seemed fond of Harriet, might talk to the doctor. This lady listened to Harriet's request with sympathy, and set off to see Dr. Norcom that very day.

Harriet saw the lady leave the house when she came home with her young mistress from school. The afternoon wore on, however, and Dr. Norcom did not summon her. She watched him at dinner as she served him his meal. He ate greedily, and ordered her about, but he gave no sign that anything unusual had happened. Harriet lay awake all night, expecting Dr. Norcom to burst into her room at any moment.

When the next morning came, Dr. Norcom sent word that he wanted to see her in his study. As she approached, she saw the door half opened, and she stood for a moment looking at him from the hall. He was seated by his desk, in front of a window, and the light cut across his face. Harriet hated him. She loathed his red face when he shoved it up close to hers and the feel of his pale eyes on her. As she looked at him, she could not believe that here was the man who claimed the right to rule her. She opened the door slowly, then walked in to stand in the middle of the room. She hoped that she appeared calm.

He watched her enter with narrowed eyes.

"So you want to be married, do you?" he asked.

"Yes, sir," she replied.

"Well, I'll soon convince you whether I am your master, or the fellow you honor so highly. If you *must* have a husband, you may take up with one of my slaves."

"Don't you suppose, sir," Harriet said, taking one step forward, "that a slave can have some preference in marrying? Do you suppose that all men are alike to her?"

"Do you love this nigger?" he burst out.

"Yes, sir," she answered.

"How dare you tell me so!" Dr. Norcom shouted, rising out of his chair. Harriet started back, and, noticing this, Dr. Norcom seemed to change his mind, and reseated himself. "I supposed you thought more of yourself," he said.

"It is right and honorable for us to love each other," Harriet replied. "He would not love me if he did not believe me to be a virtuous woman."

Without warning, Dr. Norcom sprang out of his chair and struck Harriet across the face. This was the first time he had ever hit her, and she was stunned.

"I despise you," she said after a full minute. "You have no right to do as you like with me."

"Silence!" he cried, throwing his arms straight up. "By heavens girl, you go too far." Clenching his fists, Dr. Norcom struggled to regain his composure. "You have been the plague of my life," he spit out at her. "Never let me hear that fellow's name again. If I ever know of your speaking to him, I will cowhide you both; and if I catch him lurking about here, I will shoot him as soon as I would a dog."

For two weeks following this encounter, Dr. Norcom watched Harriet in silence, like a wolf eyeing its prey. One day, he handed her a note. It said that he planned to go to Louisiana in the autumn, and to take her with him along with some other slaves. If she agreed, and deserved to be well treated, he would never mistreat her.

Although they never went, Harriet knew that it was in Dr. Norcom's power to send her anywhere he wanted. He could not control her thoughts and feelings, so he sought to control her movements.

She tried to imagine how all this would end. How could the young man marry her, knowing that his wife and his children would be slaves? He was like Harriet's father—proud with an independent heart. He would be miserable having to stand by and watch his family abused, with no power to protect them.

When Harriet urged the young man to go to the Free States and leave her behind, she knew that her wish for love could never come true. He still hoped to return to the South to buy her. But hope for this was dead in Harriet. She felt that the only people she had left to love were her grandmother and brother. Yet what was to prevent Dr. Norcom from having her brother sold away from her?

Among themselves, slaves often spoke in wonder about the North—how different it was from the South, how many people there opposed slavery, how one could live free. Because she could read, Harriet was often asked if the newspapers published anything about white people in the North who were working to free the slaves. In the

kitchens, fields, and cabins, slaves exchanged stories about runaways who had been seen by friends traveling in the North, and who carried messages to their anxious relatives back home. Or they speculated about what happened to others who had simply disappeared above the Mason-Dixon line.

Harriet and her brother talked often about how they would get to the North. But Harriet was watched closely, and they had no money for their escape. Besides, their grandmother, who had seen a son recaptured and tortured for trying to flee, was against running away. God will provide, her grandmother advised. Harriet tried to believe her. But Dr. Norcom's persecution intensified, and Harriet felt she had to do *something* for herself.

"And now, reader, I come to a period in my unhappy life, which I would gladly forget if I could," Harriet wrote of this time. "The remembrance fills me with sorrow and shame. It pains me to tell you of it; but I have promised to tell you the truth, and I will do it honestly, let it cost me what it may."

Harriet's persecution by her master and mistress was well known by their neighbors in Edenton. In fact, it was because his intentions were so obvious that Dr. Norcom may have held himself back—he did not want to lose all public standing.

One of these neighbors was a lawyer named Samuel Tredwell Sawyer, who lived on the same street as Harriet's grandmother. He had grown up in Edenton and had known Molly and her family for years.

About this time, he began stopping Harriet in the street to speak to her. He asked many questions about her master, which Harriet answered only in part. When he saw her troubled looks, he expressed sympathy. He began writing her letters, in which he mingled words of admiration and encouragement and offers of help.

Here was a dangerous choice put before her! Dr. Norcom had actually begun to build a cottage four miles from town, where he intended to force Harriet to live and where he would visit her whenever he liked. On the other side, Mr. Sawyer was offering her kind words and sympathy.

Like other slave girls, Harriet had had to grow up quickly, and she knew what Mr. Sawyer intended. She turned over and over in her mind the likely outcome of becoming involved with Mr. Sawyer. Certainly, Dr. Norcom would be furious. Yet Harriet wanted revenge for all those days and nights of terror and humiliation. Maybe Dr. Norcom would become so enraged that he would sell her, and Mr. Sawyer could buy her. If this were to happen, Harriet reasoned, perhaps she was more likely to be given her freedom. In fact, Harriet had seen other victims of Dr. Norcom sold off as soon as he tired of them, especially those slave women with his children.

But other feelings swayed her. Mr. Sawyer's singling her out in this way had inclined her heart toward him more than a little. He was not her master, and his attentions flattered her and touched her pride. She came to think that in agreeing to Mr. Sawyer's proposals, she could avoid some of the brutality and cruelty that so many other slave women faced.

For months, she told no one of her involvement with Mr. Sawyer. Neither her brother nor her grandmother knew. She dreaded telling her grandmother, especially. Molly Horniblow had taken much pride in raising her daughters and granddaughters to resist being dragged down by slavery. Harriet knew she would not be forgiven.

But in a strange way, she was eager to tell Dr. Norcom. After all these years, she felt a surge of power in being able to hurt him. Then one day Dr. Norcom called her into his study to tell her that her cottage was ready.

"That may be, but I will never enter it," Harriet told him.

"I have heard enough of such talk as that," he answered. "You shall go, if you are carried by force; and you shall remain there."

"I will never go there," Harriet replied. "In a few months I will be a mother."

Dr. Norcom stared at her in silence. Then, without saying a word, he left the house. To her surprise, Harriet felt miserable. There was no triumph in destroying Dr. Norcom's plans. Now Harriet knew she had to tell her family. They would soon hear of it from Norcom.

When she came to her grandmother's gate, Harriet hesitated. She feared her grandmother's rejection—it would feel like a turning away of her ancestors, her parents. Her grandmother gestured toward her, but Harriet could not make herself speak. Instead she sat down in the shade of a tree by her door and, taking out her mother's silver thimble, she began to sew. She felt her grandmother's eyes upon her, but neither spoke.

Just then, Mrs. Norcom stormed into Molly's yard. When she saw Harriet, she began pounding the gate like a madwoman. Mrs. Norcom called Harriet horrible names, and accused her of being pregnant with her husband's child.

Harriet's worst fears were realized when, hearing the mistress's words, Molly ran toward Harriet. "You are a disgrace to your dead mother," she yelled at the weeping girl. She tore from Harriet's fingers the silver thimble and her mother's wedding ring, which she wore. "Go away!" she cried, "and never come to my house again."

Tears were streaming down her grandmother's face. But Harriet could think of nothing to say. She felt the disgrace more than anyone.

Harriet struggled to her feet. She reached for her grandmother's hand, but the old woman pulled back. Fighting back tears, Harriet turned and ran into the street. People paused to look at the stricken girl hurrying by. She walked and walked without thinking until exhaustion overtook her. By the time she stopped, she was five miles out of town. She sat down on a tree stump. By then it was night, and the stars shone brightly through the branches of the tree. How calm and far away they looked.

When Harriet awoke, the dew was rising, and she felt a chill coming over her entire body. Is this what it feels like to die? she wondered. As the sky lightened, birds began chirping wildly. Suddenly, she was surrounded by sound. Heaving herself to her feet, Harriet started walking once more. This time, though, she headed toward the house of a woman who had been her mother's friend. The woman took her in and listened to her tale. Then, she told Harriet to send for her grandmother.

Harriet waited several days in suspense for her grandmother, all the while praying that Molly would come, yet doubting that she would. But she came, and, in tears, Harriet told her of her desperation, how in the crisis of Dr. Norcom's persecution, she saw no other way but to accept Mr. Sawyer.

Molly listened, her eyes lowered. When Harriet was through, Molly laid her hand on her head, though she did not look her in the face. "Poor child," she murmured. "Poor child."

This was not forgiveness, Harriet knew, but it was pity and love. And for this Harriet was grateful.

Harriet lived with her grandmother until her child was born. The baby, a boy, weighed only four pounds at birth. But he survived. Harriet named him Joseph, after her beloved uncle who had escaped when she was a child.

After Joseph was born, Harriet remained at her grandmother's. Dr. Norcom's frustration that Harriet was even slightly out of his power was great indeed. But Mrs. Norcom swore to kill Harriet if she came into her house, and no one doubted that she would.

Still Harriet never felt far from Dr. Norcom's control. The doctor frequently used her brother, John, who worked as his medical assistant and shop-boy, to bring unwanted messages and letters to her. By working with the doctor, John had learned to make medicines and to use a leech cup to draw blood from sick patients. He had also taught himself to read and write.

Harriet's affection for her brother made Dr. Norcom jealous, for he could not stand the thought that Harriet loved anyone else. He hoped that forcing John to take messages to his sister might make her hate and mistrust her brother. But instead, it caused them to pity each other in their shared misery.

In revenge, the doctor became especially cruel to John. The boy could do nothing right, and the doctor yelled at him constantly. Dr. Norcom also visited Harriet himself. Although he hadn't been able to get Harriet to tell him who the father of her child was, he forbade her ever to see this man again. One day, in his fury, he threw Harriet down a flight of stairs. She was so bruised that she could not turn over in her bed for weeks.

Meanwhile, a great uproar was taking place across the South. On the nights of August 21 and 22 in 1831, a slave named Nat Turner and his followers had killed fifty-five white people in Southampton County, Virginia. This was only forty miles upstream from Edenton, and word of the massacre spread quickly through the town. Within a month, nineteen slaves belonging to ten Edenton slave-holders were arrested for conspiring to revolt against their masters. They were found not guilty, but the disease of terror and fury had taken hold of the white South.

Fearing slave uprisings, white Southerners banded together into armed gangs to terrorize slaves and free blacks alike. Most of the raiders were poor whites, who could not afford to own slaves themselves but seemed to take special pleasure in this chance to exert their power over black people. They seemed to hate free blacks especially, whom they regarded as far more threatening than slaves.

Throughout the South, these white patrols burst into the homes and cabins of the blacks, tearing apart their belongings and robbing them of what little they had. Often the raiders hid gunshot and powder in the homes of blacks so that they could accuse them of rebellion and conspiracy to kill whites. Then they would drag the poor victims out into the square where they would whip and beat them. Many black men, women, and children fled into the woods, trying to avoid the onslaught.

Not long after Nat Turner's uprising, Harriet heard that white men from around Edenton were planning a raid on their neighborhood. She knew they were fairly safe from any real danger; they had many white friends in the neighborhood who would protect them. Still, with her grandmother, she hid her letters, money, silver, and other valuables.

At sunrise one morning, scores of white men began pouring into Edenton from all sides. Harriet watched from her window. The men were dressed in military uniforms and carried muskets, picks, shovels, and whatever other weapons were at hand. Drummers and fifers played military music, as if the men were soldiers at war.

Harriet soon heard the tramp of feet outside her door. The next instant the door was shoved open, and in piled a group of ragged men. They stood in the middle of the hallway, muskets raised, looking like starved dogs.

Bursting into motion, they began grabbing at everything they could reach. They flung open drawers and closets. They searched through every trunk and box in the house, turning the contents out onto the floor. At a cry from one of the soldiers, several pounced upon some drawers that held a few silver coins. When Harriet stepped forward to interfere, one of the soldiers pushed her back, exclaiming angrily, "What d'ye foller us fur? D'ye s'pose white folks is come to steal?"

Meanwhile, another had found a letter written to Harriet. He waved it in the air in delight, announcing that this proved that Harriet was plotting against whites. He raced with his find to the captain to read it, since he, himself, could not read. The captain of this band was a Mr. Litch, a wealthy slaveholder notorious for his cruelty. Glancing at the paper, he saw it to be covered with poetry, sent to Harriet by a friend. The fact that this slave could read maddened the captain. He tore the letter to bits. "Bring me all your letters!" he barked.

Harriet refused to budge. Then, suddenly, another cry came up from the kitchen. One of the men had found some silver spoons in the closet where Molly kept the many jars of preserves she made for the white women in town. One soldier began helping himself to one of the jars. Another joined in, and soon they were opening up all of the preserves, tasting and dumping the jam on the ground. Harriet ran in and snatched a jar from one of the men's hands. She could not stand by and watch her grandmother's work destroyed.

Eventually the men grew impatient and pushed their way into the garden. They turned up flowers and bushes with their rifle butts, shouting and swearing at those "half-free" blacks. They poked at the two cows her grandmother kept for milk. Then, cursing the family and declaring they should be burned out of their home, the captain reluctantly ordered his men to leave. They had found nothing.

When the commotion surrounding Nat Turner's revolt eventually died down, the slaveholders increased their efforts to teach their slaves religion in the hope that this would encourage them to obedience. Harriet attended several church meetings that slaveholders organized for slaves, but did not think much of them. She thought it was amusing for slaveholders to preach that it was a great sin for slaves to disobey their masters. She also noticed how Dr. Norcom, who about this time joined an Episcopal church, seemed to become even more vicious afterward.

Harriet preferred the Methodist religious meetings. Slaves would clap, sing, stomp, and shout. Their chants and songs gave them hope. They sang about being free in the next world. But their songs could easily be heard to express the slaves' yearning to see their masters punished and to run up North to freedom.

Ole Satan thought he had a mighty aim;
He missed my soul, and caught my sins.
Cry Amen, cry Amen, cry Amen to God!

He took my sins upon his back;
Went muttering and grumbling down to hell.
Cry Amen, cry Amen, cry Amen to God!

Ole Satan's church is here below.
Up to God's free church I hope to go.
Cry Amen, cry Amen, cry Amen to God.

Harriet continued her relationship with Mr. Sawyer, and soon she was pregnant again. Dr. Norcom was beside himself with rage when he found out. He grabbed Harriet by her long hair and, with a sharp scissors, cut it all off, hurling insults and swearing at her the entire time.

Although Harriet tried to keep Dr. Norcom's taunts from her grandmother's ears, she could not prevent the old woman from hearing. Wanting to protect her grand-daughter, Molly would raise her voice against Dr. Norcom. But this only provoked the doctor to further violence.

Finally, the day came when Harriet's second child was born. When she was told it was a girl, Harriet turned her head to the wall. Tears welled up in her eyes, and she bit her lip. She knew what awaited a girl who was born a slave. No loving mother could ever shield her from harm. As she would later write, "Slavery is terrible for men; but it is far more terrible for women."

Harriet would name her daughter Louisa, after her father's former mistress. She also gave Louisa her own father's last name, Jacobs, even though it was the name of a white man, and her family had no legal right to it. White men did not legally recognize their mixed-race offspring as their own, and they rarely gave them their names. Slaves generally took the names of their masters while they worked for them, and switched their names when they changed masters. After emancipation, when they were freed, many slaves took new names for themselves.

Several years passed, and as the children grew, Harriet's heart became heavier with dread. Dr. Norcom would often remind her that her children belonged to him, and that he was planning to sell them one day. He was a greedy man who loved money, but he loved this power he had over Harriet more, so he would not sell them right away.

Finally, the doctor offered Harriet a choice. Obey him absolutely and he would set her and her children free; but if she refused, he would send them all to his son's cotton plantation, where they would be treated like the most wretched field slaves, without the protective presence of her grandmother, Mr. Sawyer, or their other neighbors and friends.

Here was a trap, set to spring. Harriet knew that the doctor would never free her or her children. But to go to the plantation! The son would be as brutal as the father.

Before the week was out, Harriet had made up her mind: She would go to the plantation, but from there she would find a way to defeat her master and save her children, or die in the attempt. She told no one of her plans.

Her grandmother felt there was something going on, but when she asked, Harriet brushed it aside. She played a role with her brother, too, telling him that all was well. She thought they would try to talk her out of her plans, and she did not want to hurt their feelings by arguing.

When the day arrived to hear Harriet's decision, Dr. Norcom came. He said he trusted that Harriet had made a wise choice. Harriet's grandmother was close by, holding in her hand a doll she was making for Louisa. She put the doll aside, and looked at her granddaughter anxiously.

"I am ready to go to the plantation," Harriet stated.

Molly moaned, and put her hand to her heart.

"Do you know what this means for your children?" Dr. Norcom asked angrily.

"I do."

"Very well. Go to the plantation, and my curse go with you."

Harriet would write of this in her autobiography:

I had my secret hopes; but I must fight my battle alone. I had a woman's pride, and a mother's love for my children; and I resolved that out of the darkness of this hour a brighter dawn should rise for them. My master had power and law on his side; I had a determined will. There is might in each.

Early the next morning, a wagon was sent to Molly Horniblow's house to take Harriet and her children, Joseph and Louisa, to young Mr. Norcom's cotton plantation. Joseph, who was sick, remained behind; Harriet and Louisa set off on the six-mile journey.

The young Mr. Norcom was soon to be married, and Harriet was expected to make the house ready for his bride's arrival. She planned to work hard, day and night, to avoid suspicion. Harriet worked in the great house—scrubbing, sweeping, sewing, washing, carrying, churning butter—and in the garden and yard. She wanted to seem as happy as possible, but her heart was wretched all the time.

The slaves were given a weekly allowance of food every Monday evening, but the small amount of meat, herring, and corn doled out was not enough to feed hardworking people. Louisa was not used to the harsh conditions of slavery and soon broke down. Kept apart from her mother, except late at night when Harriet lay down, exhausted, beside her, and with no one to take care of her, Louisa cried herself sick each day.

Finally, one morning when the old cart was loaded with shingles to bring to town, Harriet put Louisa in it, and sent her home to Molly.

Over the next six weeks, while the Norcoms waited for the bride to come to her new home, Harriet made the twelve-mile journey back and forth several times between her grandmother's home and the plantation. Each time she visited, her two children would cling to her, dreading her departure.

All during these weeks, Harriet longed for her children. She hated to push away the hands and arms that clung to her when she said good-bye. She loved them more than life itself. But she knew that as long as they remained with her grandmother, they were out of harm's way, at least slightly.

One evening before returning to the plantation, Harriet went to the graveyard where her parents were buried. The graveyard was in the woods, and the birds were beginning to twitter in the twilight. At the head of her mother's grave stood a black tree stump—all that remained of a tree her father had planted. Her father's grave was marked by a rough wooden board, on which was written his name. But the letters were nearly erased.

Standing above the spot, Harriet prayed for guidance in what she was about to do. She knew that attempting to run for freedom was a dangerous idea, and she shuddered to think what might happen if she were caught. On her way out of the woods, she passed the old meetinghouse where, before Nat Turner's time, the slaves used to gather to pray. As she walked by, she thought she heard her father's voice calling out to her, saying, "Do not wait, till you reach freedom or the grave."

That night, she stood in her old room in Molly's house and packed up some of her belongings.

"What are you doing?" her grandmother asked, when she saw her.

"I am putting my things in order," she said.

Her grandmother grew alarmed. "Do you want to kill your old grandmother? Do you mean to leave your little helpless children? I am old now, and cannot do for your babies as I once did for you."

But Harriet replied that if she were gone, maybe their father would be able to obtain their freedom.

"Ah, my child," Molly sighed. "Don't trust too much to him. Stand by your children, and suffer with them till death. Nobody respects a mother who forsakes her children; and if you leave them, you will never have a happy moment. Try to bear a little longer. Things may turn out better than we expect."

Harriet could not break the old woman's heart, and promised not to take anything out of the house without telling her. But that night as she lay awake beside her grandmother, Harriet thought how it was going to be for the last time.

On Monday, Harriet returned to the plantation. Wednesday night she would have to act. That morning a white gentleman who had always been friendly toward her grandmother had called at the Norcom plantation.

"How do you like your new home?" he asked Harriet. "They don't think you are contented, and to-morrow they are going to bring your children to be with you. I am sorry for you, Harriet. I hope they treat you kindly."

With this warning, Harriet knew what was about to happen. The doctor was sending her children out to the plantation to be "broken in." Once there, they would be beyond her saving.

Wednesday night was quiet as Harriet went about her evening's work, passing through the great house, shutting windows and locking doors. Then she climbed the stairs to the third floor, where she waited until midnight. The hours crawled by. All that Harriet would be risking came before her eyes: the safety of her children and brother, the love of her grandmother, her own life.

At half-past midnight, she slipped downstairs like a cat. On the second floor she thought she heard a noise, and halted. Then, she tiptoed down the stairs and across the hall until she reached the parlor. She went to a window and peered out into the night.

It was so dark outside that Harriet could not see her hand in front of her. But she had not a minute to waste. She raised the window softly and leaped out into the darkness. Rain was falling, and it mixed with the sweat on her face and neck. She dropped to her knees to say a prayer. Then, making her way to the muddy road, she headed toward town.

She planned to go to her grandmother's house, then on to the house of a friend who had promised to conceal her. Her scheme was to remain hidden until Dr. Norcom had given up the search. Harriet hoped that Dr. Norcom, fearing she would return to help her children escape, would give in and sell them all to Mr. Sawyer or to another friend, rather than risk losing their value.

When she reached Molly's house, Harriet had Sally, a woman who had lived with her grandmother for years, help her hide her clothes in Sally's trunk. Harriet wanted any search party that might come after her to find her empty trunk and think she had fled Edenton. Harriet also asked Sally not to tell her grandmother.

At first, Sally urged Harriet to give up her plan. "For God's sake, don't go. Your grandmother is trying to buy you and de chillern. Mr. Sawyer was here last week. He tole her he was going away on business, but he wanted to go ahead about buying you and de chillern, and he would help her all he could. Don't run away."

But Harriet told Sally that the Norcoms were taking her children to the plantation that very day, and that they would never sell them as long as she was in their power. "Now would you advise me to go back?" she asked.

So Sally helped her and kept her secret. Before she left the house, Harriet took one last look at her children, who were sleeping quietly in their beds. They were blissfully unaware of the sorrow that would meet them when they woke up.

Harriet plunged out into the darkness and rain again. She ran until she came to the house where she was to hide.

The next morning, the younger Norcom marched into her grandmother's house asking for Harriet. Molly said she did not know where she was; as she spoke, Norcom watched her face carefully to see if she was telling the truth. "Are her children with you?" he asked, finally. "They are," Molly answered. "I am very glad to hear that," he said. "If they are here, she cannot be far off. If I find out that any of my niggers have had any thing to do with this damned business, I'll give 'em five hundred lashes."

By afternoon, Dr. Norcom had heard about Harriet's flight from his son's plantation, and his rage was uncontrollable. He barged into Molly's house and began searching through every room, as if he expected to find her behind every door or under every bed. Her empty trunk was soon discovered, which, as Harriet had hoped, led Dr. Norcom and his son to think she had taken her clothes with her. They had the constable set up a night watch over the town, and then sent men to stop all of the northbound ships and search them from top to bottom.

Before night, Dr. Norcom had printed up an advertisement offering a reward for Harriet's recapture. He posted it at every corner and for forty miles around. It offered a $300 reward for his slave, and described the runaway as "an intelligent, bright, mulatto girl, named Harriet, 21 years of age. Five feet four inches high. Dark eyes, and black hair inclined to curl; but can be made straight. Has a decayed spot on a front tooth. She can read and write, and in all probability will try to get to the Free States."

Meanwhile, Harriet had arrived at her friend's house, not far from her grandmother's. There she hid for a week, while the Norcoms' search went on around her. They soon came so close that she was sure they had found her out. When she heard their loud voices, she ran out of the house and buried herself in a thicket of bushes. She crouched there for two hours in agonizing suspense.

That night, Harriet decided to send word to her family. When they heard what had happened, they stopped trying to convince her to return to her master. They knew they must help her find another place to hide.

By this time, Harriet's escape was talked about everywhere in Edenton, in the large houses as well as in the small cottages. A white woman who had known Molly from childhood stopped by Molly's when she heard to see if Harriet was safe and to find out what she could do. She owned slaves herself but had always been a good friend to Molly and her family. She offered to conceal Harriet in her own home for a while.

Soon afterward, Harriet received a message to leave her friend's house at a certain hour and to go to a place where someone she knew would be waiting for her. Harriet did not know who had made these arrangements, but she felt sure that whoever it was really was a friend. When the appointed hour came, she wrapped her head in a piece of cloth and went to meet the person who had summoned her. There, she found Betty, an old friend, who worked as the white lady's cook.

Harriet's heart leaped up when she realized who it was who had offered to help her. Without speaking a word, she and Betty sped through back streets to the lady's house. When they were safely inside the door, Betty took Harriet's hand. "Honey, now you is safe," she said. "Dem devils ain't coming to search *dis* house."

What a change the last twenty-four hours had brought for Harriet! She could hardly follow the whirl of events. The lady soon came and led Harriet to a small, closed-off room above her own bedroom. She told Harriet that no one ever went there, and that she would keep the other girls away, and that only Betty would know of their secret.

Betty arrived shortly afterward, carrying a tray with a hot supper, while her mistress hurried downstairs to the kitchen to make sure that Betty would not be missed. Harriet, grateful and exhausted, went to sleep that night "feeling that I was for the present the most fortunate slave in town."

There was a pile of featherbeds in her room on which Harriet could lie completely concealed and keep watch of the street. From there, she could spy on Dr. Norcom as he passed everyday to and from his office. But the triumph she felt at having outwitted him soon faded. She was like a small bird watching its owner through the narrow bars of its cage. The few months that Harriet hid in the house of her white benefactress were filled with tension.

Dr. Norcom seemed to have nothing else to do but to look for Harriet and make life unbearable for her loved ones. He had her children, brother, and aunt jailed in Edenton as a way to force her family to give up information about her. The thought of this tormented Harriet. It was painful to think how much her family suffered on her account, and the burden of guilt weighed heavily upon her spirits.

Betty visited the jail frequently for news, which she would bring back to Harriet. But since she was not allowed to enter the jail, she stood outside the window while John held up Joseph and Louisa in turn for her to see. The jailor liked John and treated the children well. But Harriet's heart ached to have them released.

It was Betty who kept Harriet going through the anxious months of her isolation and confinement. Betty acted as Harriet's eyes and ears to the outside world; like a person in the desert dying for a drink of water, Harriet would greedily take in Betty's descriptions of her children.

There were many scares. One day, Dr. Norcom stopped in at her grandmother's and announced that he knew where Harriet was and that he would have her before twelve o'clock. Alarmed, Harriet's grandmother ran to tell Betty, who instantly tore upstairs to tell Harriet to get dressed quickly. Harriet obeyed, then the two women stole downstairs and across the yard into the kitchen, where Betty removed a plank from the wooden floor to reveal a narrow space, on the bottom of which was spread a buffalo skin and a piece of carpet.

"Stay dar till I sees if dey know bout you," Betty said, easing Harriet down into the hole. When Harriet lay down she had barely enough space to cover her eyes with her hands to keep the dust out. She could hear Betty overhead, walking back and forth between the fireplace and the counter, twenty times an hour. When Betty was alone, she muttered curses against Dr. Norcom. When the housemaids were there, she would draw information out of them for Harriet to hear, by repeating stories she had heard about Harriet's being in this place or that. Oh no, they would answer, she's not that much of a fool. She's in Philadelphia or New York.

When night finally fell, Betty lifted the plank to release Harriet, who was stiff from lying in one place for so long. "Come out, chile; come out," she whispered. "Dey don't know nottin 'bout you."

Another time, Harriet was sewing in her upstairs room when she heard Dr. Norcom's voice. Her blood froze.

For several terrifying minutes she believed that Dr. Norcom was going to search the house and find her. But soon Harriet learned that was not the reason for his visit. Her benefactress brought the reassuring news that Norcom was actually going to pursue Harriet in New York, where he was sure she was hiding, and that he had come to borrow five hundred dollars for his expenses. "My sister had some money to loan on interest," she told Harriet, "and he proposes to start for New York to-night. So, for the present, you see you are safe. The doctor will merely lighten his pocket hunting after the bird he has left behind."

During that month of July 1835, when the doctor was away, Harriet felt a little more at ease. She spent her time sewing, reading the Bible, or chatting with Betty, who brought her stories and good things to eat to keep up her strength. But Harriet also spent hours looking out the window, dreaming of freedom with her children. She imagined them one day living together in a home of their own in the North. It all depended on her.

As Harriet's benefactress had predicted, the doctor returned from the North at the end of July a poorer man but no wiser. He had been discouraged by his fruitless efforts. He also had borne the expense of keeping John and the children in jail these two months—he had already released Harriet's aunt because Mrs. Norcom discovered that she could not do without her. Harriet's

friends decided that now was a good time to offer Norcom money for his slaves.

One night, after everyone had gone to sleep, Harriet was sitting in her usual spot by the window, thinking of her children, when she had an unusual experience. Feeling as if some unseen presence were hovering beside her, Harriet lowered herself to her knees. Just then, a streak of moonlight lit up the floor before her, and in the strip of light appeared the forms of her two children. The vision vanished almost as soon as it had appeared, but Harriet had seen it clearly. She felt with a certainty that something was happening to her children.

Betty had not been to visit all day, but now Harriet heard her rustling outside her door. As soon as Betty entered, Harriet ran and grabbed her arm, begging her to tell her what had happened to her children.

"Lor, chile," Betty clucked, putting her arms around Harriet. "You's got de highsterics. I'll sleep wid you tonight, 'cause you'll make a noise, and ruin missis. . . . De chillern is well, and mighty happy. I seed 'em myself. Does dat satisfy you? Dar, chile, be still! Somebody vill hear you."

Anxious and weary, Harriet got no sleep that night, though Betty was sleeping soundly next to her. At dawn, Betty was up and in the kitchen. All that morning, the memory of the vision of her children haunted Harriet. Around midday, she heard the voices of two women rising up to her from downstairs. She recognized one of them as Jenny, the housemaid. Harriet put her ear against the door to hear better. The second housemaid was saying to Jenny, "Did you know that Harriet Jacobs's children was sold to the speculator yesterday? They say ole massa Norcom was might glad to see 'em drove out of town; but they say they've come back agin. I 'spect it's all their daddy's doings. They say he's bought John too. Lor' how it will take hold of ole massa!"

Harriet felt as if she were going to cry out. She ran from the door to the window and looked out. Was it true? Where were her children? Who had bought them? Were they safe? Won't Betty ever come?

It seemed hours to Harriet, though it was only several minutes, before Betty burst in, her face lit with a smile. Harriet gripped her arm and plied her with questions, the words tumbling over one another. "Lor, you foolish ting!" Betty teased, "I'se gwine to tell you all about it."

What Betty reported was better than Harriet could have imagined, short of their all being freed. Mr. Sawyer had sent a slave trader to Dr. Norcom to offer to buy her children and brother. Sawyer's offering prices were high for slaves: nine hundred dollars for John, and eight hundred apiece for the children. At first Norcom rejected the offer, but he then thought better of it, and the sale was made. Dr. Norcom did not know to whom he had sold the three, and it was not until the next day, when he went to ask Molly, that he found out that their new owner was Mr. Sawyer.

Knowing that her children were beyond Norcom's grasp brought Harriet a "season of joy and thanksgiving. It was the first time since my childhood that I had experienced any real happiness. I heard of the old doctor's threats, but they no longer had the same power to trouble me. The darkest cloud that hung over my life had rolled away." It seemed that at the very time of Harriet's vision, her children were with their father at Molly's, celebrating their release from Norcom.

After the sale of John and the children, the doctor renewed his search for Harriet with an intensified urgency. He felt that he had been duped by the entire family, and he hated them all.

Then one day not long afterward, Harriet was in her room when she heard someone at the door, fumbling with different keys at the lock. Somebody obviously was in a hurry because the keys were dropped several times. Harriet suspected that it must be one of the housemaids who had grown suspicious because of a noise or from seeing Betty go up and down the stairs. When Betty came that evening, Harriet told her what had happened. Betty guessed right away that it was the housemaid Jenny.

Not long before, Norcom had come to suspect that Harriet was still in Edenton, and even had the house she was in searched. Fortunately, Betty had taken Harriet out of her room and hidden her under the kitchen floor before the men came to comb the house. But this latest incident merely confirmed the belief of Harriet and her friend that the house was no longer safe, and another hiding place had to be found.

As soon as she left Harriet's room, Betty went to report to her mistress that Jenny had tried to expose Harriet. Her mistress told Betty to keep Jenny busy in the kitchen until she could go to see Harriet's uncle Mark. He said he would send a friend for Harriet that very evening.

Without the slightest idea of where she was going, Harriet dressed herself in the disguise that Betty, whose husband was a sailor, had brought her—a sailor's jacket, pants, and hat. Betty gave Harriet lessons in walking like a sailor—"ricketty"—with her hands in her pockets. Then Betty handed Harriet a small bundle, hugged her, and wished her well. "Don't forget ole Betty," she added. "P'raps I'll come 'long by and by."

Harriet left the house and was met by a man named Peter, who had been her father's apprentice and whom she had not seen for years. He had been sent by Uncle Mark to escort Harriet to a boat that would be waiting. She was to stay on board until dawn, then taken to Snaky Swamp, where she was to hide until her uncle Mark came for her.

Snaky Swamp was a wild marshy growth of bamboo and briars just southwest of town, where outlaws who raided the plantations and escaped slaves often hid. Patrols looking for fugitives had to cut their way through the tangled branches.

While Harriet waited anxiously at the edge of the swamp, Peter broke a path through the brambles, then came back for her. He carried her into a seat he had made among the bamboo. The swamp was wet and smelly. Hundreds of mosquitoes swarmed all over their bodies, covering their flesh with swollen and sore bites. When daylight came, Harriet saw snakes slithering all around them. Harriet was terrified of snakes. Now she beat them back with sticks to keep them from crawling over her body.

Harriet and Peter spent the whole day in the swamp, but at night they sneaked back to the boat. At dawn they were returned to the swamp. This time, Peter had brought back tobacco to burn to keep the mosquitoes away. It worked, but it also gave Harriet a severe headache and left her nauseous. By now she was also running a high fever.

When they returned to the boat the second night, Peter, who saw how sick Harriet was, promised that she would go home tonight, even "if the devil himself was on patrol." She was told that John and her uncle Mark had made a hiding place for her in her grandmother's house. She could not imagine how this was possible, and Peter was reluctant to say.

When at last the rowboat took them ashore, Harriet was beginning to feel a little better. Disguised in her sailor's clothes, her face blackened with charcoal, she walked beside Peter through the streets of Edenton, passing neighbors and friends without being recognized. She even brushed by Mr. Sawyer, who did not know her.

"You must make the most of this walk," Peter told her; "for you may not have another very soon." Harriet was puzzled, but she soon came to understand what he meant.

Molly's house had seven rooms—two upstairs and five below. On the west side of the house was a piazza, and on the east side were two rooms, with a hallway leading to the center of the house. One of these rooms was used as a storeroom. Its ceiling was made of boards, above which was a shingled roof that rose at an angle to a point. Between the ceiling and roof was a crawl space, from three and a half feet to four feet in height.

In one corner of the storeroom, Uncle Mark had built a cupboard that attached to the ceiling. Behind the board at the very top of the cupboard he had cut a trapdoor leading up to the crawl space. It was so small and cleverly done that it was completely invisible to anyone who did not know exactly where to look.

It was here, in this crawl space, that Harriet Jacobs spent seven years hidden by her family from Dr. Norcom,

until, having made sure of her children's freedom, she escaped to the North. She would call it her "loop-hole of retreat," but she also came to think of it as her "prison."

Harriet's family hurried her into this hiding place as soon as she arrived that night with Peter. The air in the crawl space was stifling hot, with no light. The mice and rats had scurried away when she first intruded upon what had been their exclusive territory, but they shortly became used to her, and were soon scampering all over. In addition, tiny red insects bit her skin all over, making it burn as if pricked by a million lit matches.

The space was long enough for Harriet to lie down, but she could not turn over without knocking her head. After a while, she developed a stiffness and numbness in her arms and legs from which she would suffer the rest of her life. Occasionally, her family would close all the doors and windows and let her come down and walk around, so that she would not become crippled entirely. But such occasions were rare. Her meals were passed through the trapdoor. Her grandmother also brought her herb teas and some cooling medicines that made the sting from the insect bites go away.

There was also a small hole broken into the wall of one of the upper-story rooms through which Harriet could speak to her grandmother, uncle, or brother. Eventually, Harriet bored three holes into an outer wall, through which she could get a little light and air. This allowed her to read her Bible and sew, and she found that being able to stitch clothes or toys for Joseph and Louisa made her feel useful and less isolated. But most important, through these holes she could actually watch her children.

Joseph and Louisa did not know where their mother was, though Dr. Norcom tried to bribe them with small gifts to tell him what they heard at home. But for Harriet, the fragmented glimpses she caught of them through the holes and the sound of their voices brought her comfort.

Even so, more than once, she had to lie listening without moving to her children's heartbreaking cries when something had gone wrong. These were the hardest times for the slave mother's tortured heart. One day she heard Joseph scream, and when she looked through her peephole she saw him standing in the street, drenched in blood from being bitten by a dog. At times like these, she felt mangled by frustration, guilt, sorrow, and anger. That she should be reduced to lying in this coffin-like space, as if *she* had done something wrong!

Cut off from light, air, and exercise, chilled by cold in winter and broiled by heat in summer, Harriet fell sick often. A leaky roof, which Molly was afraid to have repaired (they worried about drawing attention to the house) also meant that Harriet's clothing and bedding were frequently drenched. When she was ill, John would visit her, bringing her medicines to try to make her well. John had developed a reputation among the slaves for his medical skills, and he had even built up a practice of his own. Now he came to tend his sister and to bring her as much solace and tenderness as was possible in her wretched condition.

John had found in Mr. Sawyer a good master, but this had not changed his loathing for slavery. Like his father, he hated slavery with all his heart. Yet feeling that his situation was so much better than Harriet's, John almost always kept his thoughts about running away to himself. But Harriet could read John's emotions in his face. She was in conflict over her wish for John to remain to look after her children and her desire for him to do what he must to free himself.

All this time, Dr. Norcom persisted in his obsessive hunt for Harriet. By the end of her second summer in hiding, he had made three trips to New York to look for her. It was also at that time that Mr. Sawyer won a seat as a North Carolina congressman, and was preparing to go to Washington.

Mr. Sawyer had not freed Harriet's children as promised, and his plans to leave Edenton worried Harriet. What would happen to them if something happened to him? Though she had followed his movements with some care, Harriet had not spoken directly to Mr. Sawyer for several years. But she felt that she needed to speak to him before he went to Washington.

The night before he was supposed to leave, Harriet slipped down through the cupboard into the storeroom. Her muscles were so weakened from lying still for so long that she could not walk. In great pain, she crawled toward the window to wait. She thought that Mr. Sawyer would probably come to say good-bye to Molly.

Soon, she heard him outside.

"Stop one moment, and let me speak for my children," she whispered. She heard him gasp and step away. Then for a few moments, she heard nothing. She sank down hard against a barrel. It came over her suddenly that he might have grown unfeeling about his own children.

But moments later he returned. "Who called me?" he said. Harriet identified herself. "Oh, Harriet. I knew your voice, but I was afraid to answer, lest my friend should hear you. Why do you come here? Is it possible you risk yourself in this house? They are mad to allow it. I shall expect to hear that you are all ruined."

Harriet had not wanted him to know where she was hiding, for that might endanger him if Norcom should pressure him for information. Now, she told him only that she had come to speak to him about her children. "I want nothing for myself," she said. "All I ask is, that you will free my children, or authorize some friend to do it, before you go."

Without hesitating, he promised he would do what she wanted. He also said he would make arrangements for Harriet to be purchased as well.

Harriet had to be carried back to her hiding place that night. The little strength that she had to complete her mission had vanished after Mr. Sawyer left, and she sank, helpless, to the floor, where she lay until her uncle Mark found her.

Three more years passed with grueling slowness. Harriet continued to feel as if she were in a duel of wits with Dr. Norcom, who seemed bent on hunting her down until either he or she were dead. Again, Harriet sent for her old friend Peter to help her trick Dr. Norcom. This time she asked for a New York City newspaper so that she could find out some street names and addresses, then composed two letters—one to Dr. Norcom and the other to her grandmother—for Peter to take with him to New York and mail. That way, they would be postmarked as having been sent from the North, and Dr. Norcom could only conclude that she was there. The plan worked.

During those years, Mr. Sawyer, who thus far had not kept his promise to free the children, spent much of his time in Washington. John was with him as his personal servant, and sent letters back to his family regularly. Reading his letters, Harriet remembered their conversations as children when John declared that he would never buy his own freedom but take it, and she wondered if he still clung to his goal. She privately believed that he would never return South, though her grand-mother had showed her Mr. Sawyer's own letter describing John's devotion to him.

It was 1838, and word came that Mr. Sawyer was planning to return in the fall with a bride. John had accompanied him on his wedding trip through Illinois, Canada, and New York. Every day, Harriet expected letters from her brother describing his travels, but none arrived. The wait was draining, and the thought that John might not return made Harriet feel utterly alone. It was John who had shared her childhood griefs and fears, and who had been a witness to her humiliation at the hands of Dr. Norcom. She dreaded losing touch with him. Her feelings about Mr. Sawyer's marriage were far more muted. It had been a long time since their relationship had ended, and she had always assumed that he would take a white wife.

On the day that Mr. Sawyer and his bride were expected in Edenton, Molly set a place at the table for her grandson, John. Harriet, too, was eager to see her brother again. But the stagecoach arrived without John. Instead, there was a letter from John a week later. It confirmed what they suspected: He had found his chance for escape in New York City and had taken it once and for all.

Harriet felt confused about John's escape. She was proud of her brother and elated by his daring. But she also missed him greatly. Reluctantly, she also admitted to herself that she partly wished he hadn't escaped, for she feared its consequences for her children.

She was afraid that because Mr. Sawyer had spent so much money on John, he might sell her children to make up for his losses. It seemed all the more likely, now that Mr. Sawyer was married, that he might want to sell off his illegitimate children to keep them away from his new wife. And if Mrs. Sawyer ever found out about the children, what might she do to them? Harriet remembered Mrs. Norcom's violent jealousy.

But not long after the Sawyers were settled, Mr. Sawyer told his wife himself. He added that the children were motherless, and she expressed a wish to meet them. This news pained and puzzled Harriet, who did not know what to make of the young wife's request. But she soon found out. The next day, Mr. Sawyer came to Molly and told her that his wife was so taken by the children that she wanted to give Louisa to her sister, who was childless, for adoption. Mrs. Sawyer would take Joseph to raise herself.

Harriet heard the news from her grandmother in disbelief. Was this to be the end of all her labor for her children? Maybe it seemed like a good thing for them, but the lesson of slavery had taught Harriet to distrust slaveholders' care for their slave children. These children were property first and foremost, however well they were treated, and would always live under the threat of being sold to strangers or willed to heirs. Harriet had only to think back on her own experience, and her mother's betrayal by her mistress.

From her hiding place, Harriet told her grandmother to go to Mr. Sawyer and tell him that the children were not motherless, and that he must remember his promise to free them. Mr. Sawyer was taken aback by Molly's urgency, as if he had no idea how circumstances might appear to the grandmother and mother. "The children are free," he told Molly. He also said they were free to go wherever Harriet wished.

"But," he added, "In my opinion, they had better be sent to the North. I don't think they are quite safe here. Dr. Norcom boasts they are still in his power. He says they were his daughter's property, and as she was not of age when they were sold, the contract is not legally binding."

Mr. Sawyer's proposal was to send Louisa immediately to some of his relatives who were living in Brooklyn, New York. Joseph could travel to New York with his uncle Mark, whenever Mark could take him there.

And I, Harriet thought to herself when she heard these plans, will join them.

Year after year, Harriet Jacobs had lived in that crawl space yearning to be with her children in freedom. Hearing their voices or spotting them in the street was not enough. She wanted to tell them she was their mother. She feared that they would grow up with no memory of her and that they would never love her. Suffocated and shivering in her damp prison, Harriet longed to be able to walk in the sunlight and to breathe fresh air. And after Louisa was sent to Brooklyn, these desires intensified. She became increasingly restless. She could not stay inactive much longer. Every day seemed an eternity in hell.

Then the unexpected happened. Peter arrived one morning, looking excited.

"Your day has come, Harriet," he said. "I have found a chance for you to go to the Free States. You have a fortnight to decide."

At first, Harriet was overjoyed with the news. She eagerly asked Peter for details. But then she thought about Joseph, who had not yet been taken North. Seeing her hesitate, Peter urged her to go. Such a chance might never come again, he said. Joseph was free, and he could be sent to her as soon as she wanted. Harriet recognized the wisdom in this and agreed to go. But then the image of her grieving grandmother came before her. What would her grandmother feel? Who would tell her, and when?

It was never an easy decision to run away. Slaves not only risked their own lives but the lives of their loved ones. And in fleeing, they often left behind the only people they loved to go to a place where they knew no one and could trust no one.

But Harriet's uncle believed that, in the end, it would be better for Molly if Harriet left. "You cannot be blind to the fact that she is sinking under her burdens." Harriet knew this to be true, and so, agreeing to let her uncle tell her grandmother, she prepared herself to go.

Peter had arranged with the captain of a boat for Harriet to sail with him to the North. The price he had paid was what it would have cost to sail to England, but there was little bargaining to be done.

Harriet made herself ready to leave. There was nothing to take and much to leave behind. But the boat was unexpectedly delayed for several days. As she waited anxiously for word that the boat would sail, news came about the murder of a fugitive slave whose mother was an old friend of Molly's.

Such news was always horrible. But coming when it did made Molly feel certain that Harriet would meet with the same fate. Sobbing, she begged Harriet not to go to what she felt would be certain death. Harriet, whose nerves had already been tested to their limit, felt herself succumb to her grandmother's fears. Reluctantly, she agreed to give up her plan.

When Peter came for her, Harriet said she had changed her mind. Peter was disappointed and upset, but Harriet told him that she had a friend who would take her place, so the trip would not be wasted.

The next day was dark and cloudy, and still the vessel

did not sail. All the delays made Harriet more and more anxious. Each day they did not sail increased the dangers for Peter and the friend who was going in Harriet's place. On the third day, when the weather still had not changed, Molly rapped on the wall for Harriet to come down into the storeroom. Molly had also become increasingly nervous over the last several days. As Harriet watched, Molly wrung her hands in anxiety, trembling and sobbing out her fears that they all would be caught and killed.

Suddenly, a voice called out from the piazza. "Whar is you, aunt Molly?"

Without thinking, Molly opened the door. Harriet immediately ducked behind a barrel. In stepped Jenny, the housemaid who had once before tried to entrap Harriet. "I's bin huntin ebery whar for you," she said. "My missis wants you to send her some crackers."

Recovering herself, Molly left the room quickly, taking Jenny with her to count crackers. She locked the door behind her. But Harriet, in a sweat, was sure that Jenny had seen her. In a few minutes, her grandmother came back in.

"Poor child," she said, drawing Harriet out from behind the barrel. "My carelessness has ruined you. The boat ain't gone yet. Get ready immediately, and go. . . . I ain't got another word to say against it now; for there's no telling what may happen this day."

Harriet would leave, but she wanted to see her son first. When Louisa was sent to Brooklyn, Harriet had insisted on her daughter being brought to her so she could say good-bye. It had been more painful in some ways, because they had been separated all those years, and then to have to part again compounded the sense of loss. Now, with Joseph, Harriet expected the same heartbreaking scene. But to her surprise, Joseph told her that he had known for weeks that she was hiding. And now he was glad she was going away, where she would be safe from capture.

Harriet held him close and told him to take care of her grandmother, and some day he would come to her in the North. Then she turned and saw Molly holding out a small bag of money. Harriet tried to get her to keep part of it. But Molly insisted that her granddaughter take it all. She wanted her to be taken care of in case she were sick or starving. Then she took Harriet by the hand. "Let us pray," she said. They knelt down, Harriet gripping Joseph with one arm, her other wrapped around her grandmother's shoulders.

When dusk came, Harriet was ready to go. This time there would be no turning back.

She found Peter waiting for her in the street. She did not look back at her grandmother's house. Pulling her shawl over her head, she followed Peter hurriedly to the wharf.

Harriet Jacobs put her pen aside, and leaned back in her chair. Her arms were stiff and her legs were numb. She had been at her writing desk for hours after putting the Willis children to bed. If she went to bed now, she would probably be able to have two or three hours of sleep before she had to wake up to feed the baby.

She glanced at the mosquitoes buzzing near the light. She thought about what she still wanted to write. How the desire to be in the light and warmth of freedom is so strong that a slave would rather die than languish in the dark pit of slavery. How, by the time she arrived in New York, she had learned that colored people were not allowed to ride in first-class train cars with white people. How she had found her daughter in New York, and then had been found by John. She thought fondly of the first Mrs. Willis, who had been so kind to her when she needed it. Harriet recalled the first weeks she lived with the Willises, taking care of their baby daughter, Imogen. It seemed so long ago. Now Mrs. Willis was dead, Imogen was fifteen, and Mr. Willis was remarried. So many people gone, she thought. Her grandmother and uncle Mark. So many tender memories, mixed up with the bitter taste of slavery.

Harriet got up slowly from her desk and began to walk awkwardly around the room. She tried to straighten her back, with her hands pressed against her waist. She found herself thinking about Dr. Norcom, and a frown came over her brow. The Norcoms had pursued her even after her escape to the North. Her young mistress had married and with her husband had come after Harriet to try to recapture her, claiming that she was still her property. The Fugitive Slave Act of 1850 had made it perfectly legal for fugitive slaves to be seized in the Free States and sent back to slavery.

The so-called Free States, Harriet thought, shaking her head. Finally, the husband had offered to allow her to buy her freedom. Thinking of this, Harriet shook with rage. She would never buy what was hers by right!

To calm herself, Harriet returned to her desk to tidy up. She straightened out the manuscript, lining up the edges of the pages neatly. Then she tied the manuscript with its blue ribbon and put it back into the bottom drawer. She placed the ink and pen into another drawer. Finally, she took the sealed envelope in her hand. She looked at the name of her friend, "Mrs. Amy Post," which she had written out neatly above the address. She recalled how her head had reeled when she read the letter from Mrs. Willis telling her that she had bought Harriet her freedom. How the words had struck her like a blow! So, she had been sold at last!

Harriet suddenly felt a knot between her shoulders. She reached behind her back to try to massage the cramp. Yes, she remembered that letter. Was it already five years ago? Riding home that afternoon, she had the sweet feel-

ing for the first time in her life that she had nothing to fear from anyone she might come across in the street.

Harriet carried the lamp to the door. She paused, and glanced back around the room. It was a pretty room, and she had done what she could to make it feel like home. But it was not her true home, because her children were not there. And four million Americans were still enslaved. Much remained to be done.

EPILOGUE

At the time Harriet Jacobs decided she wanted the story of her life as a slave to become known, she had never written anything longer than a letter. In 1852 she turned to Harriet Beecher Stowe, whose just-published *Uncle Tom's Cabin* was a bestseller, to ask Stowe to write her story. But Stowe decided that she wanted to include Jacobs's account as part of her own new project, *The Key to Uncle Tom's Cabin*. When Jacobs heard this, she became determined to write her book herself. After practicing her skills as a writer in letters she sent to the *New York Tribune*, Harriet Jacobs began her autobiography. It took her five years to finish.

Jacobs first tried to sell her manuscript to a publisher in England. But this plan failed. Then, early in 1861, with the help of African-American abolitionist William C. Nell and white abolitionist Lydia Maria Child, Jacobs published the book herself. Reviews in the abolitionist and African-American press made Jacobs famous in abolitionist circles.

Several months later the Civil War broke out, and Jacobs turned her energies to a second public career. Because she was known, Jacobs was able to approach Northern antislavery women for money and supplies for the "contrabands"—newly freed slaves who had flocked behind Union lines into Washington, D. C. and Alexandria, Virginia, from farther South. In 1863, Harriet Jacobs and her daughter, Louisa, went to Alexandria to offer emergency health care and to establish the Jacobs Free School for the children of the refugees. Throughout the war, Harriet Jacobs and Louisa reported on their work with the refugees in the Northern press, and in England, where Harriet's autobiography was published in 1862. In 1866, after the end of the war, they moved to Savannah, Georgia, where they continued to work to provide health care and education for the freedpeople.

Thereafter, Harriet Jacobs devoted her life to the welfare of African-American people. There is not much known about her son and brother. But Louisa accompanied her mother in the effort to help their people. Working on behalf of newly freed African Americans often proved dangerous. By the late 1860s the Ku Klux Klan had begun their campaign of terror against black institutions. In 1868, in the face of increasing violence, Harriet and Louisa left the South to return to Boston. Settling in Cambridge for several years, Harriet Jacobs ran a boarding house for Harvard students and faculty.

They eventually returned to Washington, D.C., to continue to work among the poor freedmen and women. In 1892, Jacobs sold her grandmother's house and lot in Edenton, property that her family had managed to have her inherit. When in 1896 the National Association of Colored Women met in Washington, D.C., Louisa Jacobs attended.

Harriet Jacobs died the following spring, in 1897, at her home in Washington. She was buried in Mt. Auburn Cemetery in Cambridge, Massachusetts. Her daughter, Louisa, is buried beside her.

BIBLIOGRAPHY

All the dialogue in this book was taken from Harriet Jacobs's autobiography, *Incidents in the Life of a Slave Girl*. The pseudonyms used in the autobiography appear here as the real names.

Hine, Darlene Clark, Elsa Barkely Brown, and Rosalyn Terborg-Penn, eds. *Black Women in America: A Historical Encyclopedia*. Bloomington: Indiana University Press, 1993.

Jacobs, Harriet. *Incidents in ther Life of a Slave Girl: Written by Herself* (1861). Edited by Jean Fagan Yellin. Cambridge, MA: Harvard University Press, 1987

...ohn S. "A True Tale of Slavery." *The Lei-*
...ur: A Family Journal of Instruction and
...on. London. No. 476 (1861): 85-87; 108-
...5-127; 139-141.

Yellin, Jean Fagan. "Harriet Jacobs's Family
History."*American Literature.* 66:4 (December
1994). 765-767.

ABOUT THE AUTHOR AND ILLUSTRATOR

Jennifer Fleischner is an associate professor of English at the State University of New York at Albany. She has told the story of Harriet Jacobs before, in her book *Mastering Slavery: Memory, Family, and Identity in Women's Slave Narratives*, which contains a chapter on Jacobs. Jennifer Fleischner is also the author of *The Apaches: People of the Southwest* and *The Inuit: People of the Arctic*, both titles from Millbrook's Native Americans series.

Melanie Reim is an artist living and working in New York City. Her prints, paintings, and collages have been exhibited in solo and group shows and are included in many private collections. In addition to her career as an illustrator, Melanie teaches illustration at The Fashion Institute of Technology in New York City.